Caterpillar Capers

Louise Spilsbury

Published 2011 by
A&C Black Publishers Ltd.
36 Soho Square, London, W1D 3QY

www.acblack.com

ISBN   HB 978-1-4081-3387-3
          PB 978-1-4081-3386-6

Text copyright © 2010 Louise Spilsbury

Acknowledgements

The publishers would like to thank the following for their kind permission to reproduce their photographs:

Cover: Shutterstock
Pages: Dreamstime: Nikhil Gangavane 3, 10, Cathy Keifer 11, Photowitch 19, Xiaobin Qiu 17, Mykola Velychko 18, Amy Walters 21, Helen Worthington 14; Shutterstock: Airn 13, Hagit Berkovich 4, Alexander Chelmodeev 1, 15, Cathy Keifer 16, Varina and Jay Patel 20, Sue Robinson 7, Antti Sompinmäki 8, Luna Vandoorne 6, Maryunin Yury Vasilevich 12, Vblinov 5, Bershadsky Yuri 9.

Contents

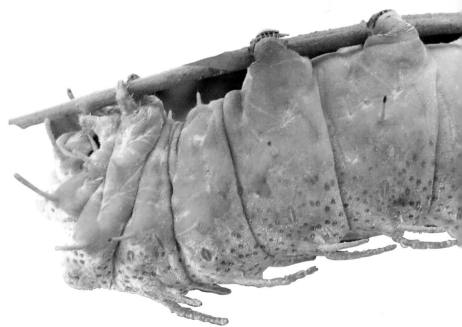

Starting Out

I started life as a tiny **egg**.
Then I became a **caterpillar**
and grew bigger and bigger.

What happened next?

I didn't just get bigger – I changed
into something new! What do you think
I changed into? Find out in my story.

Some caterpillars
are very spiky.

4

Antenna

Can't see!

Caterpillars can't see well, so they use **antennae** to feel their way around.

Guess what I will be?

My Egg

My egg was very small. In fact, it was so tiny that it was only as big as this full stop.

Sticky eggs

My mother stuck my egg onto a leaf to stop it from falling off and rolling away. Then I began to grow safely inside the egg.

My egg looked just like these.

All different

Caterpillar eggs come in different sizes and colours. Most are **oval**, but some are round.

Stick around!

I Hatched

When it was time to **hatch**, I ate a big hole in the egg. Then I slowly crawled out of the hole.

Hungry caterpillar

I was very hungry so I ate the rest of the egg, then I started to eat the leaf. I ate and ate, and grew and grew. Soon I had eaten nearly all the leaf!

chomp, chomp

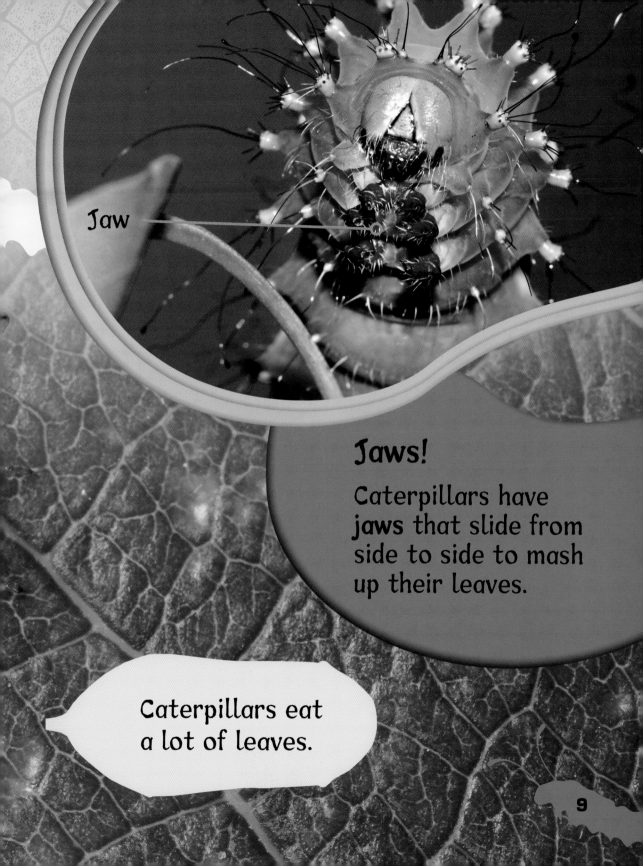

Jaw

Jaws!

Caterpillars have **jaws** that slide from side to side to mash up their leaves.

Caterpillars eat a lot of leaves.

Growing Up

I grew so much that I became far too big and fat for my skin. When the skin felt too tight, I just wriggled out of it.

New skin

Underneath I had a new, stretchier skin. My new skin felt a little damp at first, but it soon dried out in the sun.

Hold tight!

All change

When caterpillars change skins it is called **moulting**. Caterpillars grow and moult four times.

New skin

Old skin

Caterpillars grow very quickly.

In Hiding

When I was a caterpillar I had to hide. Animals, such as birds and spiders, try to catch caterpillars – then they eat them up.

Being green

I was lucky – no birds ate me. I was the same colour as the leaf I lived on, so when I kept still, the birds couldn't see me.

Happy camping

Some caterpillars make tents to hide in. They build them from **silk** they make.

Unlucky!

Birds eat some caterpillars.

On the Move

When I was a caterpillar, I often moved about in the dark. Birds could not see me moving then, so I could go wherever I wanted to.

Heave-ho

I pulled myself along on my legs. First I pulled the back legs up to the front legs, then I moved the front legs forwards.

Caterpillars can walk upside-down.

Hooked up

Some caterpillars have hooks on their legs that help them to hold on to things.

Yikes!

Hook

Time to Change

After four weeks as a caterpillar, I found a safe place to rest. Next I made a sticky pad, and then I hung upside-down from it.

Hard case

Then I moulted for the last time. My new skin became a hard, green case, and I started to change inside it.

Hold tight!

Stay inside

A caterpillar stays inside its hard, green case and changes for about two weeks.

Caterpillars grow a hard case.

Butterfly!

When I came out of my hard, green case I had changed into something beautiful – a **butterfly!**

Here I come...
First my head and legs popped out of the case, then I pulled out my body. It was very hard work. Then I stretched out my amazing, colourful wings.

Look at me!

Butterflies are beautiful.

Super scales

Butterfly wings have lots of tiny, square **scales**.

19

Flying and Feeding

Now I fly from flower to flower looking for **nectar**. It is a juice flowers make – and I drink it.

More caterpillar capers

Soon it will be time for me to lay my own eggs. Then the caterpillars that hatch from the eggs will enjoy their own capers!

Sip
Sip

Party insect

A butterfly's long tongue curls and uncurls like a party blower.

Long tongue

Butterflies drink with their tongues.

Glossary

antennae long, thin parts on an animal's head. The animal uses the parts to feel its way around.

caterpillar creature with a long, wriggly body and lots of legs. Caterpillars turn into butterflies.

egg round or oval case in which a young caterpillar grows. Eggs are laid by female butterflies.

hatch when a baby creature breaks out of its egg

jaws parts of the body that open and shut the mouth

moulting when an animal sheds its old skin

nectar sweet juice made by flowers

oval long, circular shape

scales tiny, hard parts that make up a creature's skin

silk smooth, delicate material

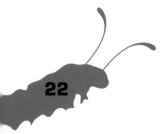

Further Reading

Websites

Find out more about how caterpillars change into butterflies at:
www.butterfly-guide.co.uk/life/larva.htm

Find out which caterpillars are in your garden at:
www.uksafari.com/caterpillars.htm

Books

Caterpillar by Karen Hartley, Chris Macro, and Phillip Taylor, Heinemann Library (2006).

Caterpillars and Butterflies by Stephanie Turnbull, Usborne (2006).

From Caterpillar to Butterfly by Anita Ganeri, Heinemann Library (2006).

The Caterpillar Story by Alex Ramsay and Paul Humphrey, Evans Brothers (2005).

Index

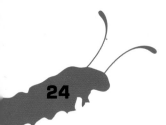